OFFICIAL FORTNITE

THE CHRONICLE 2023

CONTENTS

YOUR BATTLE BEGINS!

Where will your next Fortnite adventure take you? Whether you enjoy dropping from the Battle Bus as a solo player or like to team up with your squad, the action on the Island is never ending.

So choose your landing spot, grab a weapon, and let's get your journey started!

MEET YOUR MATCH

TIME TO TAKE ON THE FIGHT

Fortnite offers a thrilling experience to its millions of fans every day. It's a world where the battle for Victory Royale rages, with twists and turns around every corner. Out of the 100 players gliding from the sky, who will be the hero? Who can ride out the Storm, make those crucial choices, and go all the way? It's up to you to decide your own Fortnite fate. Good luck, gamers!

CROWNING GLORY!

Nothing is sweeter than seeing your battle skills totally boss the Island—a precious Victory Royale is a moment to remember. You can wear your Victory Crown with pride, knowing that you've conquered your opponents in style.

FORTNITE
FACTS

In Chapter 3 Season 1, the Pizza Party item arrived as a tasty restorative treat that boosted Health and Shield simultaneously. Share a whole pie with the squad, or take some slices with you on the go when hunger strikes!

Fortnite's announcement trailer was revealed at the Video Game Awards (VGAs) in 2011.

Players donated a staggering 1 billion Bars so that the two-player operated Salvaged B.R.U.T.E. could come into play in Chapter 2 Season 8.

In the popular Impostors game mode, the Impostor could briefly disguise all players in the Peely Outfit.

Released ahead of Halloween in Chapter 2 Season 8, the Tricks and Treats Bundle provided over 10,000 customization options for your Outfit.

When tornadoes came to the Island in Chapter 3, the Tornado Week event greatly increased the chances of encountering one. The wind was certainly at your back.

The Shopping Cart was the Island's first vehicle, appearing in Chapter 1 Season 4.

The first Limited Time Mode (LTM) in Battle Royale was 50v50 in Chapter 1 Season 1.

Enjoy gobbling up a special birthday cake each year when Fortnite Battle Royale celebrates its creation on September 26!

To increase the chance of being struck by lightning and getting a temporary speed boost, players could dive into a body of water beneath the dark cloud or climb to the highest land point under it.

Klombos, which are giant but gentle creatures, love to snack but will often sneeze out items after they fill up!

The funny Diamond Hanz Outfit was released on April Fool's Day 2021.

EYE-CATCHING OUTFITS

SHOW STYLE BY DRESSING TO IMPRESS

Make heads turn around the map when you're decked out in an awesome Outfit. The Item Shop and Battle Pass always offer new opportunities to pick up a fresh look, from battle-ready combat gear to slick suits, streetwise costumes, futuristic fashions, and much more. Here are just some of the fresh new options to choose from. Which will you add to your locker?

BACK IN FASHION

Some Outfits may return to the Item Shop for a limited time. Keep checking in so you don't miss the chance to collect one of your favorites!

GUMBO

Rarity: Epic
Set: Chew It Yourself
In-game description: "Synthetic flavors, authentic attitude."
Released in: Chapter 3 Season 1

AZUKI

Rarity: Rare
Set: Nyanjitsu
In-game description:
"Wandering warrior destined to end the Whiskeria Wars."
Released in: Chapter 3 Season 1

ABSENZ

Rarity: Rare
Set: Voidlander
In-game description: "Leave only destruction in your absence."
Released in: Chapter 3 Season 1

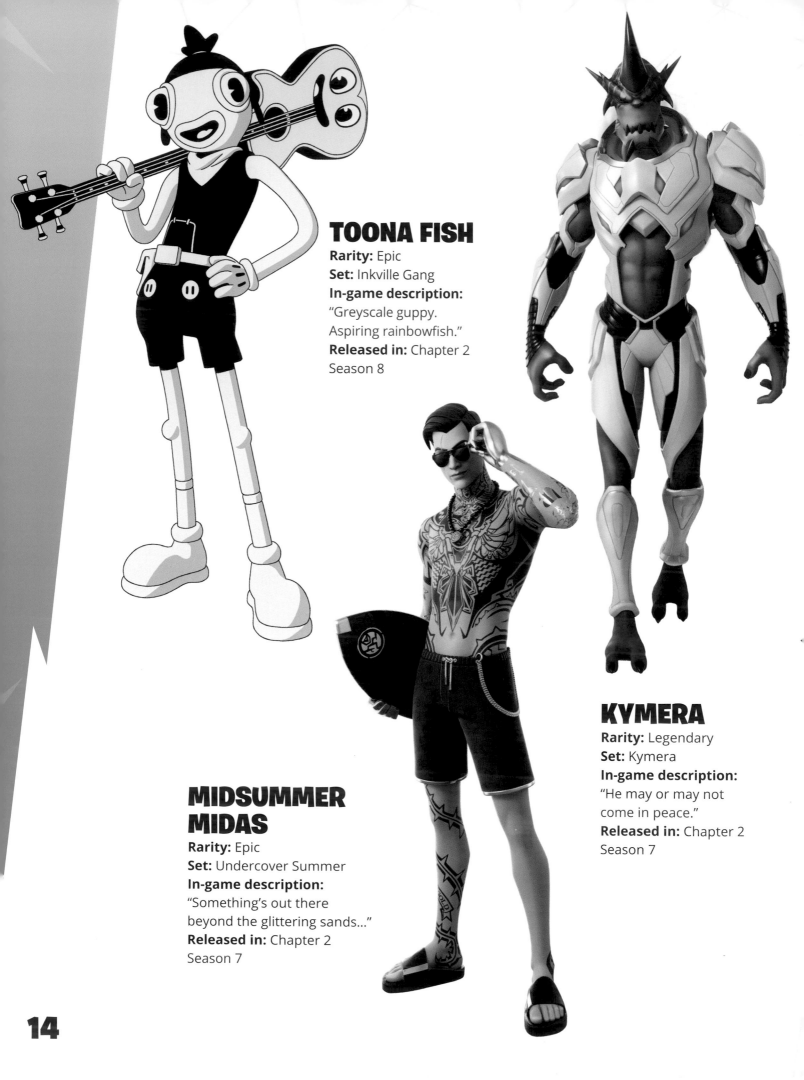

TOONA FISH

Rarity: Epic
Set: Inkville Gang
In-game description:
"Greyscale guppy.
Aspiring rainbowfish."
Released in: Chapter 2
Season 8

MIDSUMMER MIDAS

Rarity: Epic
Set: Undercover Summer
In-game description:
"Something's out there
beyond the glittering sands..."
Released in: Chapter 2
Season 7

KYMERA

Rarity: Legendary
Set: Kymera
In-game description:
"He may or may not
come in peace."
Released in: Chapter 2
Season 7

DOCTOR SLONE

Rarity: Epic
Set: IO Inquest
In-game description:
//REDACTED//
Released in: Chapter 2
Season 7

CHARLOTTE

Rarity: Epic
Set: Hagiri
In-game description: "Your typical transforming, monster-slaying teen with a possessed sword."
Released in: Chapter 2 Season 8

FABIO SPARKLEMANE

Rarity: Epic
Set: Unicorn Flakes!!!
In-game description:
"The official mascot of Unicorn Flakes."
Released in: Chapter 2
Season 8

POLAR PEELY

Series: Frozen
Set: Winterfest '21
In-game description: "That's one cool banana."
Released in: Chapter 3 Season 1

CRZ-8

Rarity: Epic
Set: Tech Future
In-game description: "Hiding in the city's darkest pockets."
Released in: Chapter 2 Season 8

TOON MEOWSCLES

Rarity: Rare
Set: Inkville Gang
In-game description: "Toon'd up for maximum cattitude."
Released in: Chapter 2 Season 6

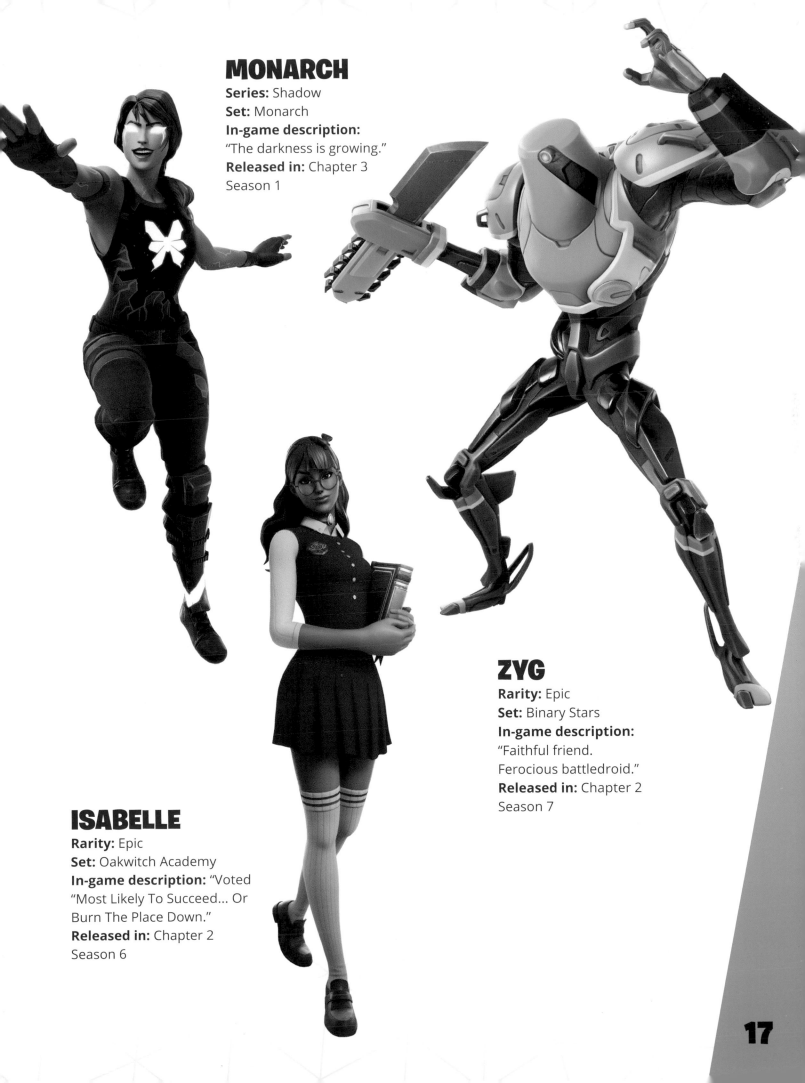

MONARCH

Series: Shadow
Set: Monarch
In-game description:
"The darkness is growing."
Released in: Chapter 3
Season 1

ZYG

Rarity: Epic
Set: Binary Stars
In-game description:
"Faithful friend.
Ferocious battledroid."
Released in: Chapter 2
Season 7

ISABELLE

Rarity: Epic
Set: Oakwitch Academy
In-game description: "Voted
"Most Likely To Succeed... Or
Burn The Place Down."
Released in: Chapter 2
Season 6

CREATE YOUR OUTFIT

BACK BLING

NAME: ....

SKETCH THAT DREAM LOOK

You've probably seen hundreds of memorable Fortnite Outfits, and now it's time to create your own unique look. Sketch your own ideas in these boxes for an Outfit that will give you a striking presence on the Island. Don't forget to draw your Back Bling, Harvesting Tool, and Glider too. Now can you come up with some cool names for your creations?

HARVESTING TOOL

NAME: ....

GLIDER

NAME: ....

OUTFIT

NAME: ....

SPIRE ASSASSIN

BRUTUS

MAVE

RIPPLEY

TOUR THE ISLAND

The ever-changing Fortnite map keeps gamers of all abilities on their toes and ready for a new challenge. Take a look at these iconic Points of Interest, locations, and landmarks. How well do you know your way round the Island?

CAMP CUDDLE

First seen: Chapter 3 Season 1
Location: West
Good for: A dive in the lake. Camp Cuddle is also home to Characters such as Cuddle Team Leader and Metal Team Leader.

SHIFTY SHAFTS

First seen: Chapter 1 Season 2
Location: North
Good for: Going underground. The mines of Shifty Shafts reveal Chests and can provide a place to escape enemies.

TILTED TOWERS

First seen: Chapter 1 Season 2
Location: Central
Good for: A blast from the past! Tilted Towers returned in Chapter 3 Season 1, complete with its much-loved clock tower and urban excursions.

THE JONESES

First seen: Chapter 3 Season 1
Location: Southeast
Good for: Running into Bunker Jonesy among the green space of this location. The watchtower is a helpful spot to scan below you.

BUTTER BARN

First seen: Chapter 2 Season 5
Location: Southwest
Good for: Meeting Mancake, plus picking up lovely loot and Slurp Barrels. Butter Barn saw a welcome return in Chapter 3 Season 1.

LOOT LAKE

First seen: Chapter 1 Season 1
Location: Central
Good for: Fishing. Loot Lake reappeared on the map in Chapter 3 Season 1, this time with a small island in the center.

CONDO CANYON

First seen: Chapter 3 Season 1
Location: South/southeast
Good for: A comfortable existence, perhaps? Condo Canyon was called a place for "cozy living" upon its release!

CONEY CROSSROADS

First seen: Chapter 3 Season 1
Location: Central
Good for: A Battle Royale rendezvous as Coney Crossroads sees paths from the east, south, and west meet. Several buildings to scope out, too.

THE TEMPLE

First seen: Chapter 3 Season 1
Location: Northeast
Good for: Looking back in time. The ancient stone designs of the pyramids reveal a colorful past, but keep eyes open for Chests and loot.

MORE FORTNITE FAVES...

CHONKER'S SPEEDWAY

SANCTUARY

IMPOSSIBLE ROCK

OUTFIT OUTLINE QUIZ

WHO'S LURKING IN THE SHADOWS?

Would you know the difference between Manic and Mancake if you were to meet one of them on a dark night? Put your Fortnite knowledge to the test by identifying these fiendish forms!

1
A. TEEF
B. DOGGO
C. HEIST

2
A. INFERNO
B. THE BRAT
C. 8-BALL VS SCRATCH

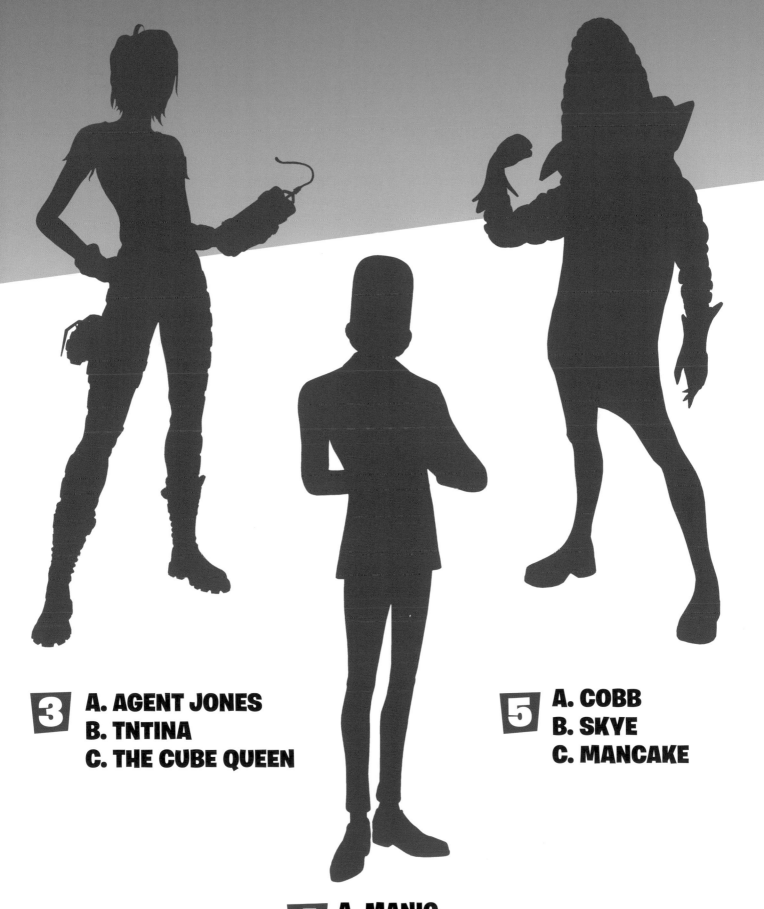

3
A. AGENT JONES
B. TNTINA
C. THE CUBE QUEEN

5
A. COBB
B. SKYE
C. MANCAKE

4
A. MANIC
B. RUBY
C. BRAINSTORM

LOADOUT LOOK

WHICH WEAPON WILL YOU CHOOSE?

Whatever trigger you have your finger on, it's essential to get the maximum from the weapon at your disposal. The range of awesome items you can have in your loadout gives you plenty of options to take down opponents. Check out these weapons as you target being the last player standing.

RANGER ASSAULT RIFLE

Described as being "made for distance" when it appeared in Chapter 3 Season 1, the Ranger Assault Rifle is ideal for mid and long-range shooting. Keep it packed with medium ammo and you'll get awesome results!

COMBAT DUO

The Combat class of weapons made its first appearance in Chapter 2 Season 8 with the Combat Assault Rifle. The Combat Pistol followed soon after.

STRIKER PUMP SHOTGUN

Some players like to have a "shottie" in their loadout to really help with their close-range combats. The Striker Pump Shotgun deals high burst damage and is definitely a desired loadout option!

GRENADE LAUNCHER

After a long time away, the Grenade Launcher returned in Chapter 3 Season 1. These projectiles now explode after their first bounce and fire more directly at the target. Very handy indeed!

HUNTER BOLT-ACTION SNIPER

Get ready for a damaging strike from way out. The Hunter Bolt-Action Sniper deals three shots in a clip, giving you a second and a third chance just in case you don't land the first!

STINGER SMG

Deal high-level damage to both opponents and structures with the Stinger SMG. At medium range this weapon, which debuted in Chapter 3 Season 1, is a master, so use it wisely.

AUTO SHOTGUN

While not having as high damage per shot (DPS) as the Striker Pump, the Auto Shotgun has a faster fire rate and reloads two shells at a time. It serves up serious firepower and delivers impressive outcomes.

SHADOW TRACKER

As another sought-after Exotic, the Shadow Tracker's party trick is marking the opposition's position and highlighting it to the rest of the squad. That's a very cool team-based ability.

GRENADES

Ever reliable and with a long history in Fortnite, Grenades get the job done when it comes to inflicting damage to players and buildings from a safe distance. Throw them in when you get the opportunity.

SIDEARM PISTOL

"Trusty" is a great way to describe this discreet weapon which should never be underestimated by the user or their opponent. Accurate with good medium-range damage.

BOOM SNIPER RIFLE

It's easy to become attached to this long-range weapon. The Exotic rarity Boom Sniper Rifle fires clingers, which stick to your target and then explode. Fancy sticking around to see the results?

MK-SEVEN ASSAULT RIFLE

What's special about this medium-to-long-range weapon is that it's an Assault Rifle with a sight you can use while aiming. Align a target with the sight's red dot and—boom!—job done!

MACHINE PISTOL

A welcome addition to the loot pool in Chapter 3 Season 1, the Machine Pistol brings battles up close and personal! With it in hand, try to get up close to your opponent to reduce the impact of its inaccuracy and make the most of the Machine Pistol's firepower.

PRIMAL FLAME BOW

Making a surprise return as part of Bownanza Week in Chapter 3 Season 1, the Primal Flame Bow is a hot weapon to have at your fingertips. If an opponent's hiding in a wooden structure then the heat will be on them!

BREATHTAKING BACK BLING

COSMETICS TO SUIT YOUR STYLE

However you play Fortnite, you can see the Back Bling that's strapped to yourself all the time, so you definitely want to enjoy the look of it! Here's some recent selections from the Item Shop and Battle Pass—which one of these has got your back?

CRIMSON CREST

First seen: Chapter 3 Season 1
Rarity: Legendary
Set: Order of the Waning Moon
A red-hot Back Bling that also comes in selectable styles of Midnight Crest and Emerald Crest.

TROT SHOT

First seen: Chapter 3 Season 1
Rarity: Epic
Set: Lloose Cannon
From the llama-inspired Lloose Cannon set, Trot Shot was unlocked as part of the Chapter 3 Season 1 Battle Pass.

KOR'S TOOLKIT

First seen: Chapter 2 Season 8
Rarity: Epic
Set: Splinter Agent
You can really make a point—or two—with this sharp-looking Back Bling from the Chapter 2 Season 8 Battle Pass. A great look for Kor.

FFROSTY

First seen: Chapter 3 Season 1
Series: Frozen
For an ultra ice-cool look, place Ffrosty on your back and head across the Island like a pro. Don't chill out too much, though.

TECH PLATE 8

First seen: Chapter 2 Season 8
Rarity: Epic
Set: Tech Future
Sport this Back Bling and you'll make a great impression on the Island. Part of the Tech Future set along with P33LY and CRZ-8.

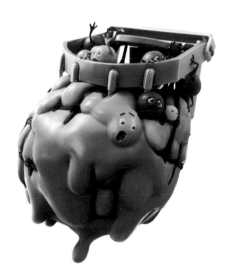

IO ORCHESTRATOR

First seen: Chapter 2 Season 7
Rarity: Epic
Set: IO Inquest
Set in black with a futuristic and edgy feel, IO Orchestrator gives you the confidence to pull the strings and lead the way in Fortnite.

GUMMY SACK

First seen: Chapter 3 Season 1
Rarity: Epic
Set: Chew It Yourself
The perfect attachment for Gumbo, this colorful Back Bling is described as "extra drippy for your busy lifestyle." Eugh!

CUBIC VORTEX

First seen: Chapter 2 Season 8
Rarity: Legendary
Set: Long Live The Queen
The Cubic Queen carries off this Back Bling with style, but it can be teamed with many other Outfits for a dynamic look.

FALL FASHION

GLIDE INTO ACTION WITH A FRESH LOOK

Get a flying start in Fortnite by deploying a great-looking Glider. From an airborne whale to giant bubblegum, check out this group of glorious designs.

THE SOARING CRESCENT

First seen: Chapter 3 Season 1
Rarity: Epic
Set: Order of the Waning Moon
Awesome in default style or the selectable styles of Azure Crescent or Emerald Crescent, this Glider makes a sky-high impression as you choose a landing spot.

WHALE SAILER

First seen: Chapter 2 Season 8
Rarity: Epic
Set: Inkville Gang
There's no gliding while hanging from this item—instead you ride on top of the whale as you descend from the Battle Bus. Pretty neat.

ROCKET SCIENCE

First seen: Chapter 2 Season 8
Rarity: Epic
Set: Astronaut P-14
Thankfully you don't need to be a rocket scientist to deploy the Rocket Science Glider. With unlockable Rose and White styles it's awesome in the air.

WOOLY MAMMOTH

First seen: Chapter 3 Season 1
Rarity: Rare
Set: Lloose Cannon
Another memorable item from this set, Wooly Mammoth uses jet-powered truck wheels to smoothly steer you to the ground.

HYPERBOARD

First seen: Chapter 2 Season 5
Rarity: Rare
Set: Y-Labs Hunter
Are you hyped for a Battle Royale? You will be after deploying the Hyperboard Glider and making a grand anime-style entrance.

WYVERN X77

First seen: Chapter 3 Season 1
Rarity: Rare
Set: Deep Future Outlaw
Spring from a Launch Pad mid-game and redeploy the WYVERN X77 Glider to show off all of its fine tech, lights, colors, and fierce form.

PROPELLER PERRY

First seen: Chapter 3 Season 1
Rarity: Epic
Set: Inkville Gang
Joining Whale Sailer as part of the Inkville Gang set, the Propeller Perry glider might cause a rough landin', mac!

BUBBLOON

First seen: Chapter 3 Season 1
Rarity: Epic
Set: Chew It Yourself
The in-game description detailed this as "Unpoppable. Unstoppable. Chewy." That just about sums up this bubblegum-tastic Glider!

BACK TO THE DRAWING BOARD
HOW TO DRAW: RONIN

Using a pencil, begin by sketching some basic lines for this Legendary Chapter 3 Outfit.

Carefully add circles and ovals to build Ronin up.

Now draw in firm body lines and begin to erase the shapes from stage two. Note Ronin's wide and powerful stance.

Refine Ronin's right arm and add his awesome swords. The cape, hood, and feet can be worked on too.

5

Spend time on face and hand details. Bring Ronin's armor to life with careful details.

6

Don't forget the lower half of this Outfit from the Order of the Waning Moon set.

7

This stage requires patience; don't be afraid to rub work out and start again. Keep your pencil sharp.

8

Clever shading and color will complete your Ronin creation.

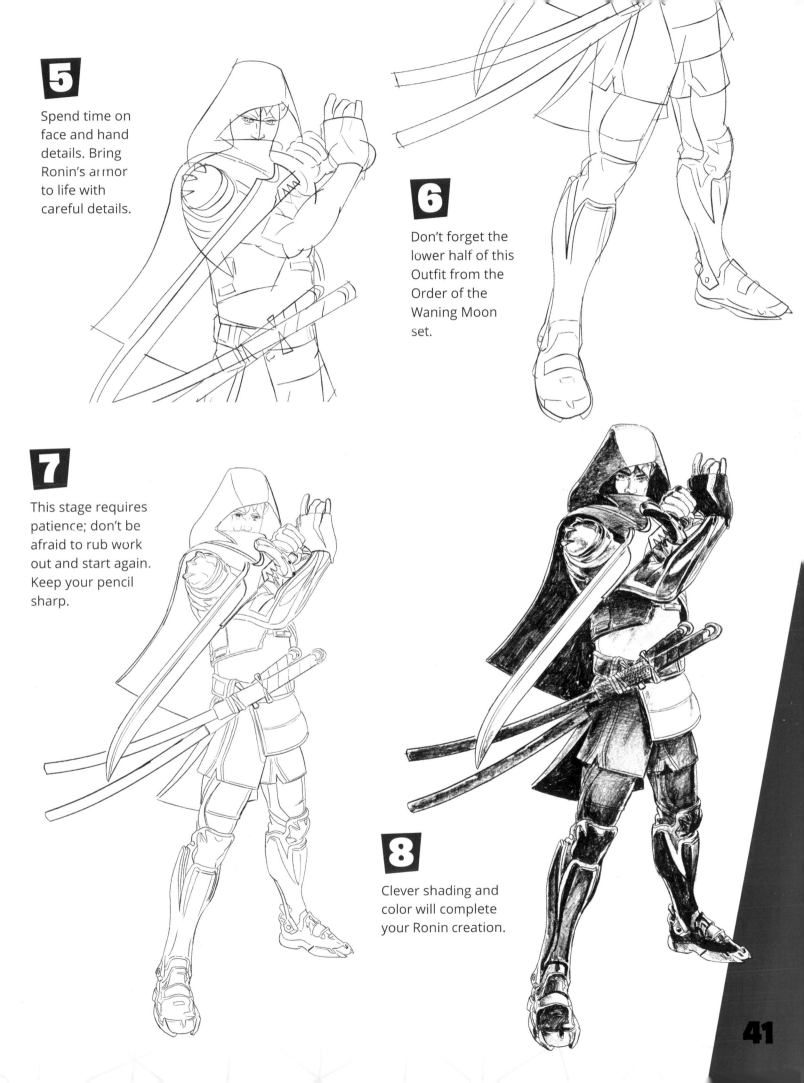

HOW TO DRAW: TARANA

1 Capture Tarana's pose with some simple pencil strokes.

2 Fill out the lines and pay attention to her arm, hip, and leg placement.

3 Add more lines and the initial details of Tarana's fingers and feet. Accurately mark the eyes and mouth.

4 Now concentrate on what she's carrying. Keep the equipment in scale to her body size.

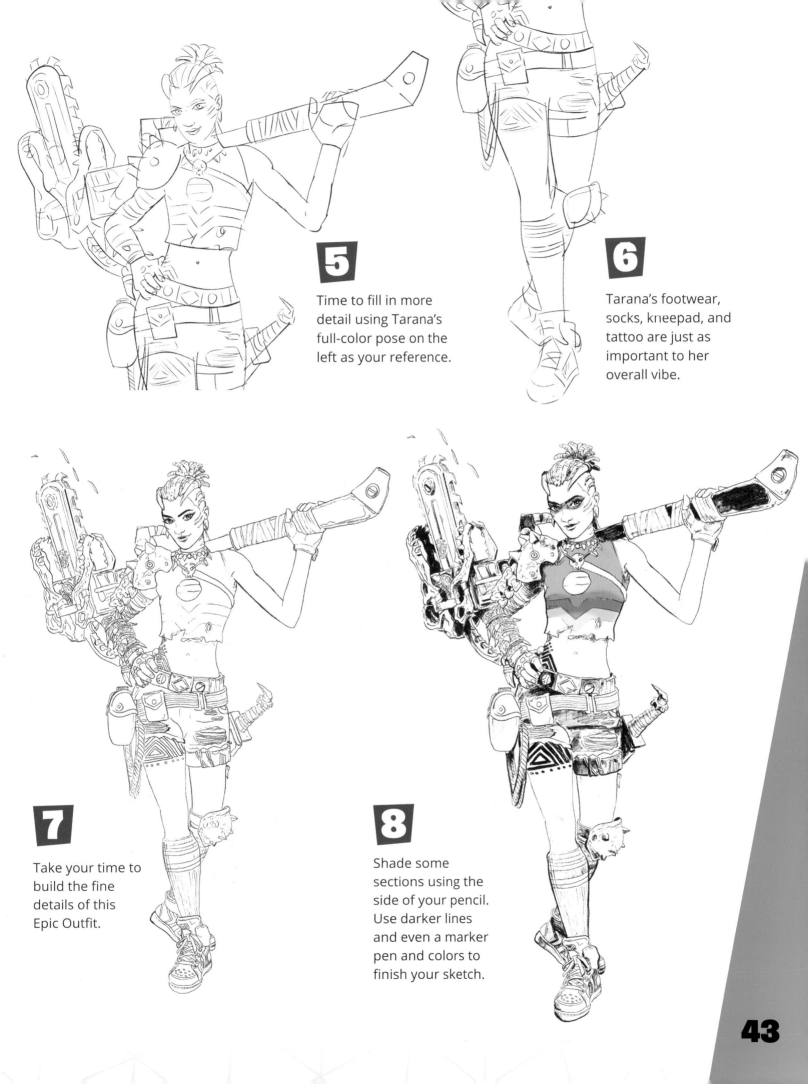

5 Time to fill in more detail using Tarana's full-color pose on the left as your reference.

6 Tarana's footwear, socks, kneepad, and tattoo are just as important to her overall vibe.

7 Take your time to build the fine details of this Epic Outfit.

8 Shade some sections using the side of your pencil. Use darker lines and even a marker pen and colors to finish your sketch.

HOW TO DRAW: POTASSIUS PEELS

1

The correct placement of Potassius Peels' right arm is particularly important as you lay out his framework.

2

As well as scoping out his torso and limbs, begin to mark how his pointy head will shape up.

3

Place the eyes and mouth and add the outline of fingers. Potassius Peels' legs are slim. Erase sketch marks that are not needed now.

4

Focus on the first shapes of his armor and footwear but don't worry about the lion features just yet.

44

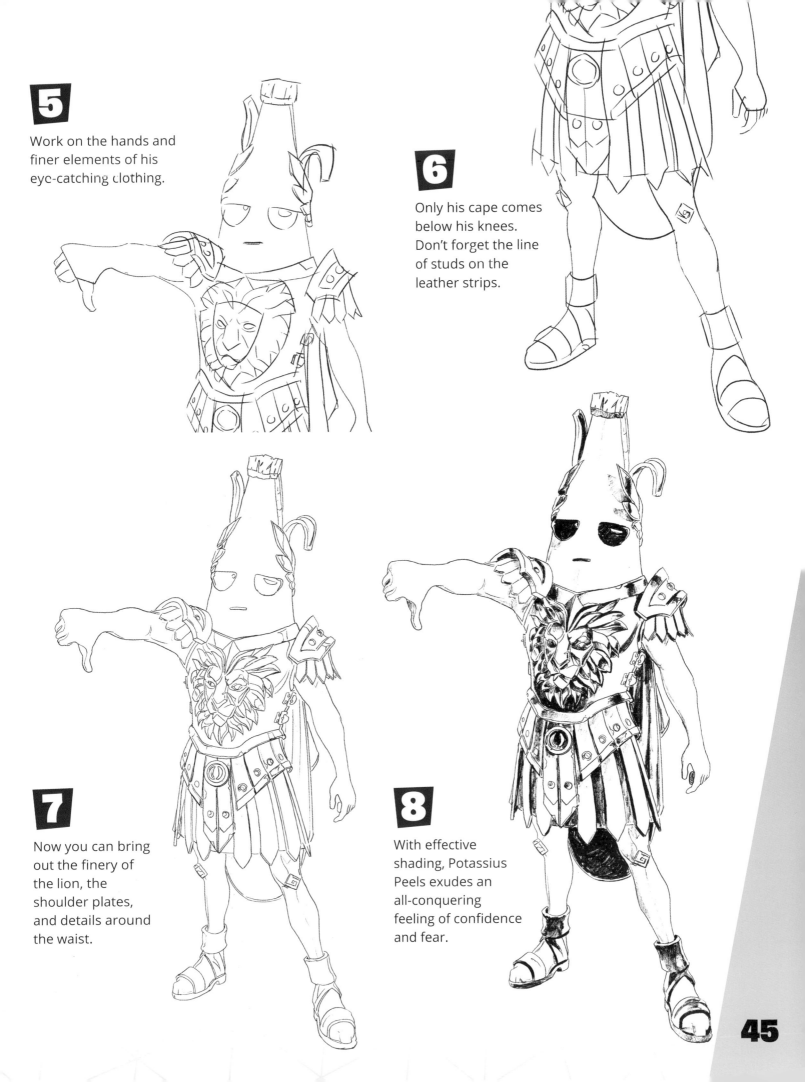

5

Work on the hands and finer elements of his eye-catching clothing.

6

Only his cape comes below his knees. Don't forget the line of studs on the leather strips.

7

Now you can bring out the finery of the lion, the shoulder plates, and details around the waist.

8

With effective shading, Potassius Peels exudes an all-conquering feeling of confidence and fear.

45

HAPPY HARVESTING

GRAB THE TOOL TO DO THE JOB

As well as customizing your Outfit, Back Bling, and Glider, there are hundreds of amazing Harvesting Tools to choose from. Pick through this top selection.

WILDERSPEAR
In-game description:
"Sharp, swift, and wild beyond measure."

SPIKEBAT
In-game description:
"Classics never die."

THE BIG SPOON
In-game description:
"Part of a balanced breakfast royale."

CHAINSAUR
In-game description:
"Sometimes you need a dinosaw."

SPIRE FLAME
In-game description:
"Aglow with mystical flame."

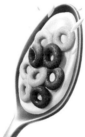

JOSIE
In-game description:
"Mancake would never leave Butter Flats without her."

TYPES OF HARVESTING TOOLS...

Harvesting Tools come in several different categories. Which ones do you prefer?

CLASSIC

Just like: Bananaxe, Dragon's Claw, Throwback Axe

SWORD

Just like: Blade of the Waning Moon, IO Eradicator, Gladius of Potassius

DUAL-WIELD

Just like: Just like: Hack & Smash, Cupid's Dagger, Party Crashers

FUTURISTIC

Just like: Storm Bolt, Razor Smash, Depth Charger

MAKE A MOVE

Show who's bossing the Island by bustin' out some special moves. Whether it's an understated action or a full-on dance demo, Emotes will get you noticed.

LIL' MONSTER

Rarity: Epic
You are instructed to "Keep on lil' truckin" when you ride the mini machine beneath you in this standout sequence.

ROLLY RIDER

Rarity: Rare
You've just got to roll with it here as you jump on the ball and master an amazing balancing act. Impressive to see in action.

CROWNING ACHIEVEMENT

Rarity: Epic
First you need a Victory Crown, and then you can detail the Crowning Achievement Emote after you win a match. Total respect for this display.

MWAHAHA

Rarity: Uncommon
The scary sounds combined with the menacing laugh makes for an imposing Emote. Unleash this to send out a strong signal.

FLAKE SHAKE

Rarity: Epic
A built-in emote for everyone's favorite cereal mascot, Fabio Sparklemane, Flake Shake's sugary goodness sends you into a frenzy of dance and song. Everybody get some Unicorn Flakes!

DOUBLE DANCE

High Five was the first synched (two-player) Emote in Battle Royale, as part of the Chapter 2 Season 1 Battle Pass.

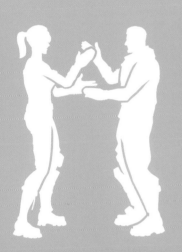

MEMBERS ONLY

Rarity: Rare
With some smart hand clapping followed by the magical appearance of a big yellow heart, Members Only is very eye-catching.

ZOMBIE SHAMBLES

Rarity: Uncommon
Leaning back, arms raised, mouth open, and legs flailing—that's pretty much the essence of the frightening Zombie Shambles move!

EGG DROP SCOOP

Rarity: Uncommon
The instruction is to simply "Exit through the gift basket" but placing the egg inside is trickier than you'd think. An impressive move.

LIL' ROVER

Rarity: Epic
The preferred mode of traversal for space explorer J.B. Chimpanski, Lil' Rover is the perfect emote for cruising around parts unknown. Onward to lil' discoveries!

KICK BACK

Rarity: Rare
Pull up a chair. It's time to sit back, relax, and soak in those summer rays with this chill emote.

FORTNITE QUIZ

Tackle all the questions to see how you score out of 50. There are two points for each correct answer. Good luck and good quizzing.

1. What is this Battle Royale player doing?

☐ **A.** Striding ☐ **B.** Slinking ☐ **C.** Sliding

2. Klombos eat just about anything, but this is their favorite. Can you name it?

....

3. This detail is taken from which Outfit?

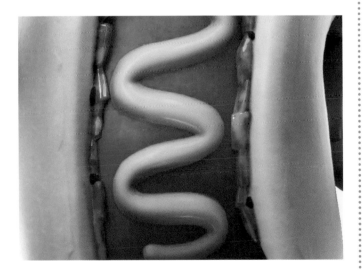

☐ **A.** The Brat ☐ **B.** Cobb ☐ **C.** Mancake

4. How many Seasons were there in Chapter 2?

....

5. If an item or feature is removed from Fortnite, it is said to have been what?

☐ **A.** Vanquished ☐ **B.** Vaulted

☐ **C.** Vanished

6. What is this Vehicle called?

....

7. Can you name the location by studying this picture?

☐ **A.** Loot Lake ☐ **B.** Tilted Towers

☐ **C.** Shifty Shafts

ANSWERS ON P. 57

8. Can you identify the Tactical Submachine Gun from these blurry weapons?

☐ **A.**

☐ **B.**

☐ **C.**

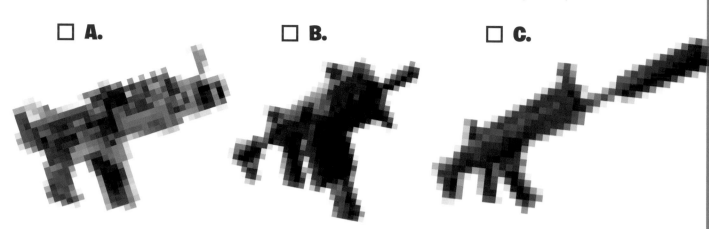

9. Which Battle Pass (name the Chapter and Season) started in October 2019?

....

10. What's the name of this Emoticon?

☐ **A.** Electro Shuffle

☐ **B.** Boogie Down

☐ **C.** Syrup Slinger

11. Which one of these locations was not in Chapter 3 Season 1?

☐ **A.** Coney Crossroads

☐ **B.** Greasy Grove

☐ **C.** Frenzy Farm

12. Whose eye is this?

....

13. How many numbers are there in a Creative Island code?

....

14. What color are Legendary weapons?

- ☐ **A.** Orange
- ☐ **B.** Yellow
- ☐ **C.** Purple

15. If Epic Games make changes and additions to Fortnite, what can it be known as?

- ☐ **A.** Fastfix
- ☐ **B.** Hotfix
- ☐ **C.** Coolfix

16. True or false? A Shield Keg can restore your squad's Shield but not that of an opponent.

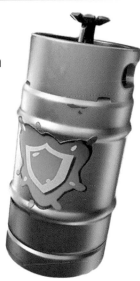

- ☐ True
- ☐ False

17. What is the seasonal event held around Halloween called?

18. Whose feet are these?

    ☐ **A.** Polar Patroller

    ☐ **B.** Fennix

    ☐ **C.** Rex

19. Epic's Picks is a cool feature in which Fortnite tab?

    ☐ **A.** Create

    ☐ **B.** Discover

    ☐ **C.** My Library

20. What is this item called?

21. When Outfits and items can be bought together in the Item Shop, what is this known as?

    ☐ **A.** Delivery

    ☐ **B.** Bundle

    ☐ **C.** Package

22. The Goalbound Set is themed around which sport?

    ☐ **A.** Hockey

    ☐ **B.** Baseball

    ☐ **C.** Soccer

23. Season and Milestone are types of what?

24. What does I.O. stand for in Fortnite Battle Royale?

25. Can you match the
correct vehicle name
to the right model?

.... Titano Mudflap

.... OG Bear

.... Victory Motors Whiplash

.... Islander Prevalent

A.

B.

C.

D.

SET IT OUT

EXPLORE THE READY-MADE ISLAND STYLES

As well as being an individual who likes to mix and match, you can also pick a set and rock the full look. Sets work on a theme, creating colors and styles that perfectly blend your Outfits with Back Blings, Gliders, Harvesting Tools, and more. Why not select a Wrap to extend your fashion to weapons and vehicles? Scan over these awesome sets and some of the Outfits and items they include.

ROYALE HEARTS SET

Outfits: Cuddle Team Leader, Love Ranger, Heartbreaker, Stoneheart, Fallen Love Ranger, Metal Team Leader
Back Blings: Love Wings, Fallen Wings, Sweetheart, Broken Heart, Warning Bow
Gliders: Bear Force One, Cuddle Cruiser, Heartspan
Harvesting Tools: Cupid's Dagger, Snuggle Swiper, Cuddle Paw

LOVELY STUFF
Watch out for Royale Hearts releases around Valentine's Day in February.

PASTEL PATROL SET

Outfits: Bunny Brawler, Rabbit Raider, Pastel, Stella
Back Blings: Eggshell, Hard Boiled
Harvesting Tools: Sprout, Carrot Stick
Wraps: Pastel Print, Spring Party

FORT KNIGHTS SET

Outfits: Ultima Knight, Royale Knight, Red Knight, Dark Red Knight, Blue Squire, Black Knight

Back Blings: Squire Shield, Red Shield, Dark Shield, Dragoncrest

Gliders: Sir Glider the Brave, Steelwing

Harvesting Tools: Axecalibur, Crimson Axe, Vanquisher

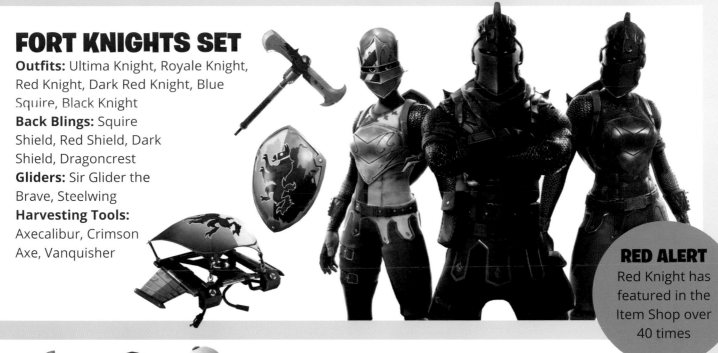

RED ALERT
Red Knight has featured in the Item Shop over 40 times

GETAWAY GANG SET

Outfits: Wild Card, Dark Wild Card, The Ace, Heist

Back Blings: Swag Bag, Tiny Totem, Cuff Case, Crystal Llama

Harvesting Tool: Crowbar

Wraps: Diamonds, Hearts, Spades, Clubs

HARDBOILED SET

Outfits: Noir, Sleuth, Gumshoe

Back Blings: Evidence Bag, Cluefinder, Confidential Case

Gliders: Viceroy Mark I

Harvesting Tool: Magnifying Axe

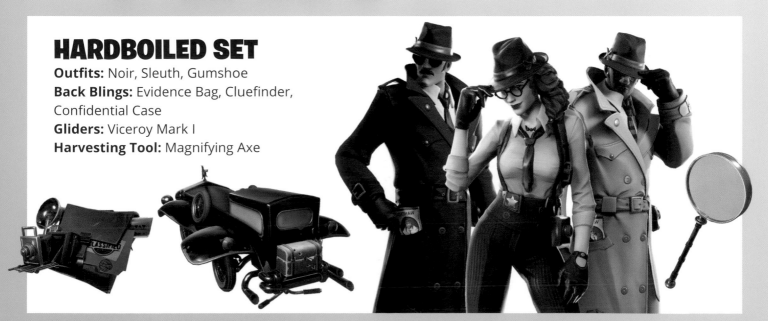

SPACE EXPLORERS SET

Outfits: Mission Specialist, Moonwalker, Dark Voyager, Leviathan, Eternal Voyager
Back Blings: Astro, Fish Tank, Gameplan
Gliders: Planetary Probe, Voyager, Orbital Shuttle, Deep Space Lander
Harvesting Tools: Cosmic Cleavers, EVA, Global Axe

MAKE SPACE
Space Explorer set has more than 25 Outfits and items in total, making it one of the biggest.

JAILBIRD SET

Outfits: Rapscallion, Scoundrel
Back Blings: Burgle Bag, Strongbox, Personal Pollinators
Glider: Starry Flight
Harvesting Tool: Nite Owl

WINTER SKI SET

Outfits: Alpine Ace, Mogul Master
Back Blings: Alpine Accessories, Mogul Ski Bag
Harvesting Tool: Ski Boot

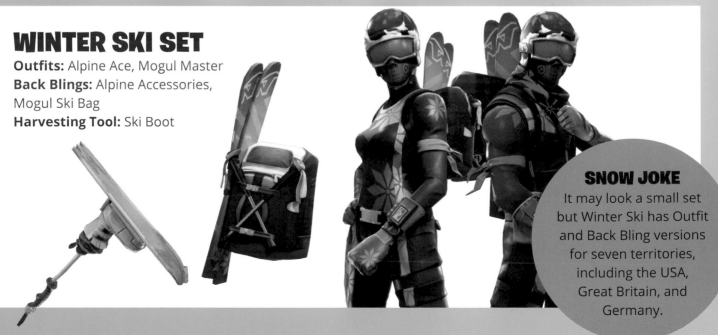

SNOW JOKE
It may look a small set but Winter Ski has Outfit and Back Bling versions for seven territories, including the USA, Great Britain, and Germany.

WESTERN WILDS

Outfits: Calamity, Deadfire, Rio Grande, Frontier
Back Blings: Shackled Stone, Grande Pack, Detonator
Harvesting Tools: Reckoning, Dark Shard, Longhorn
Contrails: Virulent Flames, Spectral Essence

WHAT A CALAMITY

Calamity was a Chapter 1 Season 6 Battle Pass Outfit and is the female counterpart to Deadfire.

SUNSHINE AND RAINBOWS SET

Outfits: Beach Bomber, Brilliant Bomber, Brite Bomber, Brite Gunner
Back Bling: Brite Bag
Gliders: Rainbow Rider, Brite Blimp
Harvesting Tools: Rainbow Smash, Brite Bashers

TECH OPS

Outfits: Tech Ops, Hypernova
Back Blings: Carbon Pack, Capacitor, Oscilloscope
Glider: Coaxial Copter
Harvesting Tools: Armature, Brute Force

FORTNITE
ORIGINALS

CLASSIC VIBES FROM THE ISLAND

Take a trip down memory lane and scan through some OG appearances from the very beginning of Fortnite Battle Royale.

DEATH VALLEY
Rarity: Epic
The in-game description says, "Whenever you need a skull on a stick, Death Valley is there for you." Enough said!

REAPER
Rarity: Rare
You're advised to "harvest resources... and souls" with this slick-looking item.

FLAMINGO
Rarity: Epic
Old-school wackiness from Fortnite's first Season.

ROADTRIP
Rarity: Uncommon
A "picnic-ready" glider with a fittingly traditional look.

AERIAL ASSAULT ONE
Rarity: Uncommon
Aerial Assault One shows off a cool military style. Perfect to team up with a Chapter 1 Season 1 Outfit.

HOT ROD
Rarity: Uncommon
Mixing bold red with flames and a skull, Hot Rod is unlike any other Glider from the first Fortnite Season.

GHOUL TROOPER

Rarity: Epic
A frightening addition at Halloween during Chapter 1 Season 1, Ghoul Trooper is a scary sight whenever she returns to the Item Shop.

TROOPER

Rarity: Uncommon
Trooper is a no-nonsense Outfit for players with just one mission: to make the end game and take Victory Royale.

MUNITIONS EXPERT

Rarity: Rare
Attention, soldier! Munitions Expert has been a force in Fortnite ever since she was released in November 2017.

SCOUT

Rarity: Uncommon
A classic combat Outfit which shows you mean business when you drop to the Island.

RENEGADE RAIDER

Rarity: Rare
Check out the combat pants, helmet, and subtle facepaints—be ready for whatever comes your way.

TRACKER

Rarity: Uncommon
Show that you're super serious about scooping the Victory Royale by dropping in as Tracker.

SKULL TROOPER

Rarity: Epic
Now with selectable styles such as green glow and gilded, Skull Trooper is as popular now as he was in 2017!

BACK IN TIME
Back Bling was introduced to Fortnite Battle Royale in Chapter 1 Season 3.

BATTLE ROYALE RECORD

KEEP TRACK OF YOUR GAME GLORY

NAME:

....

MY PLAYER NAME:

....

DATE:

....

CHAPTER & SEASON:

....

PLATFORM PLAYING ON:
- ☐ CONSOLE
- ☐ PC
- ☐ MOBILE

LOCATIONS LANDED:

....

....

....

SQUAD MEMBERS:

....

....

....

....

LOCKER:

OUTFIT:

....

GLIDER:

....

BACK BLING:

....

HARVESTING TOOL:

....

EMOTE:

....

CONTRAIL:

....

WRAP:

....

TACTICS:

....

....

....

....

....

....

....

....

....

....

....

LOADOUT:

....

....

....

....

BATTLE PASS ACHIEVEMENTS:

....

....

....

FORTNITE FAVES

FAVORITE WEAPONS:

SHOTGUN:

....

RIFLE:

....

PISTOL:

....

SUBMACHINE GUN:

....

EXPLOSIVE:

....

FAVORITE BATTLE PASS:

....

FAVORITE VEHICLES:

....

....

FAVORITE QUESTS:

....

....

....

....

FAVORITE CREATORS & STREAMERS:

....

....

....

....

FAVORITE LOCATIONS:

....

....

....

....

FAVORITE ITEMS:

....

....

....

....

FAVORITE BUILD:

....

FAVORITE ITEM SHOP PURCHASE:

....

FAVORITE CREATIVE CODES:

....

....

....

2022-2023 GAMING GOALS

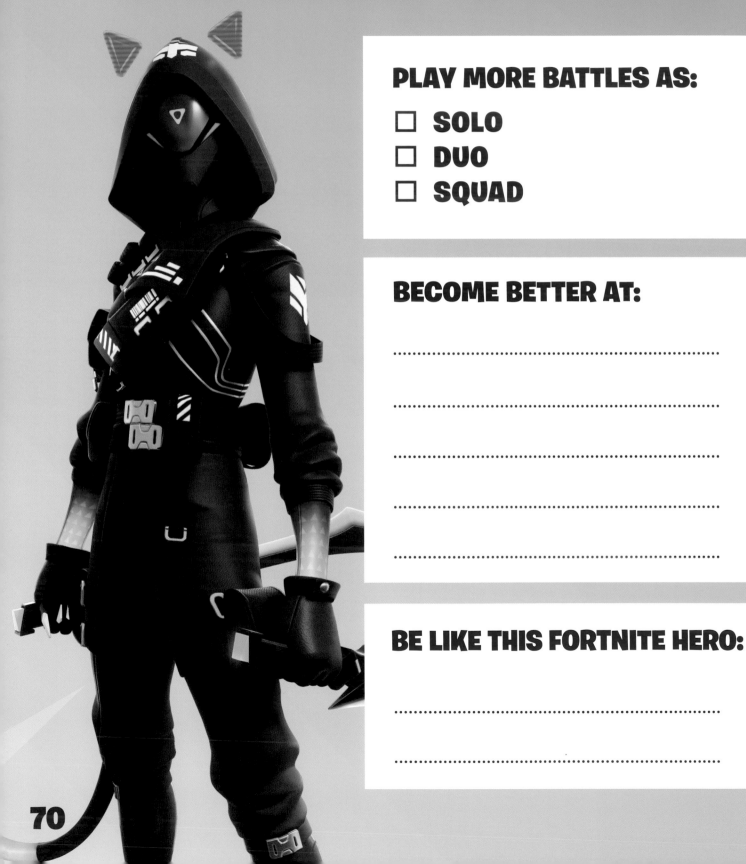

PLAY MORE BATTLES AS:
- ☐ SOLO
- ☐ DUO
- ☐ SQUAD

BECOME BETTER AT:

....

....

....

....

....

BE LIKE THIS FORTNITE HERO:

....

....

DREAM WEAPONS TO OWN:

....

....

....

DREAM GLIDERS TO OWN:

....

....

....

PERFECT ELIMINATION WOULD BE:

....

....

....

....

DREAM OUTFITS TO OWN:

....

....

....

....

....

NEW SKILLS TO MASTER:

....

....

....

....

VICTORY ROYALES TARGET:

- ☐ 0–5
- ☐ 6–20
- ☐ 21–50
- ☐ 50+

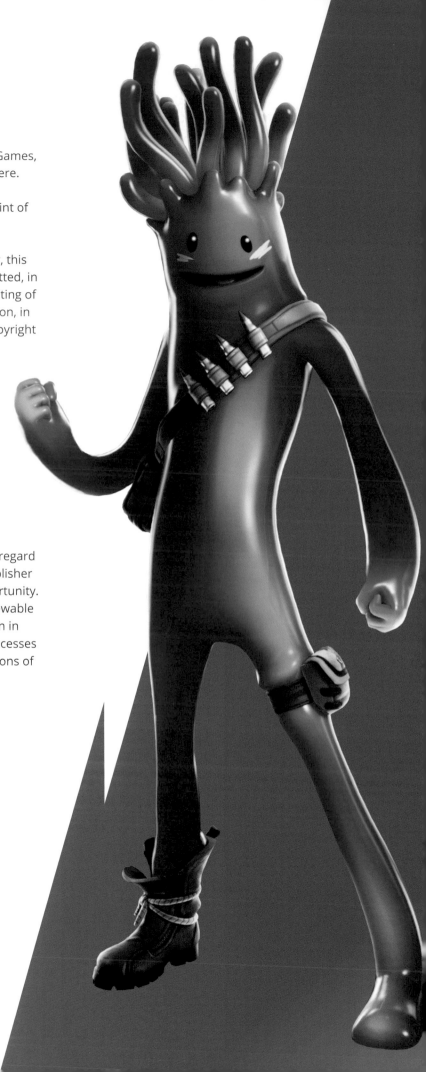

First published in the UK in 2022 by WILDFIRE an imprint of
HEADLINE PUBLISHING GROUP

Cataloguing in Publication Data is available
from the British Library
Hardback 978 14722 9740 2

Written by Kevin Pettman
Design by Amazing15
How to draw illustrations by Mike Collins
All images © Epic Games, Inc.
Printed and bound in Italy by L.E.G.O. S.p.A.

HEADLINE PUBLISHING GROUP
An Hachette UK Company
Carmelite House
50 Victoria Embankment
London, EC4 0DZ
www.headline.co.uk www.hachette.co.uk

www.epicgames.com